CHARLES SUMNER.

A EULOGY

DELIVERED BEFORE THE

FACULTY AND SOCIETIES

OF

KALAMAZOO COLLEGE,

BY HON. CHAS. S. MAY,

JUNE 16, 1874.

PUBLISHED BY ORDER OF THE SOCIETIES.

KALAMAZOO:
"DAILY TELEGRAPH" PRINTING HOUSE,
1874.

"Casting my eyes back no further than the fourth of July of the last year, when you set all the vipers of Alecto hissing, by proclaiming the Christian law of Universal Peace and Love, and then, casting them forward, perhaps not much further, but beyond my own allotted time, I see you have a mission to perform. I look from Pisgah to the Promised Land,—you must enter upon it."—*John Quincy Adams*, 1846.

"I feel bound to say that the honorable Senator from Massachusetts has, so far as his own personal fame and reputation are concerned, done enough, by the effort he has made here to-day, to place himself side by side with the first orators of antiquity, and as far ahead of any living American orator as freedom is ahead of slavery. I believe he has founded a new era to-day in the history of the politics and of the eloquence of the country; and that, in future generations, the young men of this nation will be stimulated to effort by the record of what an American Senator has this day done, to which all the appeals drawn from ancient history would be entirely inadequate."—*Hon John P. Hale, in U. S. Senate, after Mr. Sumner's speech entitled, "Freedom National—Slavery Sectional," August* 27, 1851.

"In an age of venalty and of reckless calumny, no man ever doubted the purity of his motives and the singleness of his aims; and if the august title of statesman has been deserved by any American of his age, he is that American."—*Horace Greeley*.

"We have in our possession many of MR. SUMNER's speeches, and we confess that for depth and accuracy of thought, for fullness of historical information, and for a species of gigantic morality which treads sophistry under foot, and rushes at once to the right conclusion, we know not a single orator, speaking the English tongue, who ranks as his superior.'.—*Edinburgh Journal*.

"MR. SUMNER's large ability, his careful education, his industry, his early dedication to public affairs, his power of exhaustive statement, and his pure character,—qualities rarely combined in one man,—have been the strength and pride of the Republic."—*Ralph Waldo Emerson*.

"One of those powerful intellects and noble hearts that have shown so brightly in our sister country, in the Senate of the United States. What noble eloquence! Carry his words, Sir, by the vehicle of your almost universal paper (London Times) to the press of every country and to the heart of every human being—man, woman or child—who has ever read the divine rule—'Whatsoever ye would that men should do unto you, do ye even so them."—*Lord Shaftesbury*.

EULOGY.

MR. PRESIDENT, LADIES AND GENTLEMEN:

It has been truly said that the contemplation of a great character is always an interesting and instructive work. Mankind are taught better by example than by precept, and great lives are the best teachers of great virtues. It is the mission of great men to quicken and exalt the common life of humanity by showing the almost divine possibilities of our nature, and God sends such men into the world when needed to save nations and to hold up exalted moral standards. They do not appear in regular order or in unbroken succession. Sometimes they come singly, sometimes in royal companies. Nor do all teach the same lesson or perform the same work. Some stand for religion, some for patriotism, some for heroism. Still other lofty lives, lifted above the common level, stand for warning. Not all eminence is the eminence of virtue. History has its fiery meteors and baleful comets as well as its fixed stars and orderly planets. The former blind by their brilliancy or awe by their mystery; the latter shine ever on in the serene depths with steady and invigorating light, and so teach mankind the eternal verities. And over all God watches and rules for the good of men.

You have set apart this occasion for contemplation of the life and character of a great man and you have asked me to pronounce his eulogy. It is a theme most fit to engage your attention. CHARLES SUMNER was not only an illustrious statesman and orator, but he was also a distinguished scholar. I know of no name in all our annals so well calculated to inspire the enthusiasm of young men at college or to stand for their model as his Through this shining gateway of knowledge he passed in his ardent youth; up the rugged steeps upon which your feet have entered he went with proud and conquering step, and he stands now yonder, on the immortal heights, forever beckoning you onward and upward.

Nothing could be more fit therefore, than that you should mark his name for honor and drink deep of the inspiration of his life. And for what is not fit in him who is to speak upon such a theme, I can only plead that CHARLES SUMNER was my ideal statesman; that from the days of my boyhood he has been my bright particular star among our public men, commanding always, more than any other, my admiration, my confidence, and my profoundest esteem. I have greatly honored other noble men and leaders in the struggles of our later history, but not with such honor and admiration as were called forth by the noble Senator from my native State, who ever seemed to me to stand forth on the field of conflict like the chivalrous knight of France, without fear and without reproach.

To you then, students and others connected with these societies and with this institution of learning, and to my fellow citizens here assembled, let me speak of CHARLES SUMNER. The first spontaneous utterances of grief and lament for his loss which filled all the land have ceased; the funeral pageants, so grand and impressive, have passed; the noble old Commonwealth, like a proud and sorrowing mother, has tenderly laid the ashes of her great son in her Westminster Abbey, where are gathered so many of the great and good, and the flowers of the opening summer bloom upon his grave in the beautiful Mount Auburn. In the calm which has come after the first burst of sorrow has been spent, we may now contemplate that great life in the light in which men will hereafter view it, and in which it will take its permanent place in history. I know it is the common fault of eulogy that it is too sweeping and indiscriminate; that it sees no defects or blemishes but only virtues in its subjects. But eulogy, like history, should be truthful. It should not make defects where there are none, and if the public and private life of CHARLES SUMNER was stainless and spotless, let me paint him as he was.

MR. SUMNER'S EARLY LIFE AND EDUCATION—HIS PREPARATION FOR STATESMANSHIP.

CHARLES SUMNER had a most ample preparation for the career

of statesmanship. Unlike so many of our public men who have achieved eminence, he was born to fortune and to large advantages of education. His native city was the one, of all others on the continent, most noted for intellectual culture and historic interest, and he was early admitted to all the opportunities of its famous institutions of literature and law. Its very streets were consecrated to patriotism and learning. It had been the theatre of some of the earliest and most thrilling events in the great drama of the revolution, and many of its buildings still bore the scars of the conflict. Bunker Hill and Fanieul Hall were there, the memory of Warren was a near and daily presence, and John Adams and other great leaders of the Revolution still lingered upon the scene, their venerable forms familiar upon the streets.

In the midst of such scenes and opportunities, the impressible youth of SUMNER was passed. How he improved these rich advantages the world already knows. He was early enrolled a student within the classic walls of Harvard, where he pursued his studies with enthusiastic ardor, soon evincing a peculiar love for those fields of culture which lay in the direction of his great life-work. From the college he passed to the law school, where his fine promise soon attracted the attention and secured the friendship of that eminent jurist, Judge Story, the memory of whose own great learning and ability, and vast judicial labors has been revived in the minds of his countrymen by the death of his illustrious pupil. When called to Washington by his duties upon the bench of the Supreme Court, Judge Story recommended young SUMNER to fill his place as law lecturer in the institution, which he did with marked success, and afterwards, declining a permanent chair in the law school and the still more flattering offer of a professorship in the college, he spent several years in general and wide reading of law and literature and in travel and study in Europe. Returning to Boston he commenced the practice of his profession under the most flattering auspices.

MR. SUMNER AS A LAWYER.

But he was not destined to run the career of the mere lawyer, even in the higher walks of the profession. He had mastered the noble science of the law as a part of general literature; he had given special attention to it in its relation to government and in its wider aspects as affecting the wellfare of races and of nations; in short, he had imbued his mind with its history and its philosophy. While this was noble study and acquisition for a lawyer, it was still better for the future statesman. It was better preparation for statesmanship than for practice in the courts. True, MR. SUMNER did, for more than ten years pursue the profession, arguing cases and notably filling the office of legal reporter in the District Court of the United States, over which Judge Story presided and editing, meanwhile, with great research and ability, a series of English reports, receiving from Judge Story in the meantime the high compliment that he was, at the beginning of his professional career, well fitted in legal learning to occupy a seat on the bench of the Supreme Court of the United States. But he never met the rougher experiences, the severe and sometimes rude encounters of the bar like so many eminent lawyers, and like those who achieve success in the profession, especially at the West. In this technical and practical sense Mr. SUMNER was not distinguished at the bar. Indeed it is doubtful if he ever would have made a successful jury lawyer. His mind had more breadth and strength than acuteness, his temperament was not electric and his great learning and habits of generalization would have made him unwieldy before a jury. Besides this his moral purposes were more suited to lofty themes than to the questions of private dispute with which the mere jury advocate has to deal.

But happily, he did not need to settle these questions by actual experience His private, inherited fortune placed him above that pecuniary want which has been the hard but powerful stimulus of so many noble minds. He did not, like Erskine, that foremost and greatest of advocates, feel dependent offspring tugging at his lawyer's gown for bread, but he was left free to pursue congenial studies and to follow the natural bent of his mind. Thus saved from sinking the man in the lawyer and repressing noble desires from base necessities, with learning so ample and profound, with a fine and manly presence and an eloquence at once polished, graceful and commanding, he was a public man even before he was called to fill public station; a man well and carefully fitted for the service of the State when she should need him. And so, when in

1845, after a succession of masterly addresses, he pronounced before the corporation of his native city that great oration on "The True Grandeur of Nations;" an oration which filled the country with admiration and drew answering plaudits from across the Atlantic, all the world saw that Massachusetts had a noble scholar and orator, with the highest graces of person, mind and character, with lofty aims and principles, full armed and equipped, and ready to obey her call to enter the arena of statesmanship and bear aloft her traditional standard.

HIS ELECTION TO THE SENATE.

The summons soon came. In the Spring of 1851, by a fortunate combination of parties in the Legislature, building wiser than they knew, he was elected to the Senate of the United States. The office had come unsought, though not unwelcome. During the long struggle at the State House, which lasted for months and attracted the attention of the whole country, he had daily passed to and from his office, but had never once looked in upon the contest, nor spoken to a single member upon the subject of the election. In vain over-anxious and well-meaning friends besought him to do this. He stood firm, and no word of importunity or impatience escaped him. And when at last the position was his, it had come without solicitation and without pledges. It is doubtful if a United States Senator has ever since been elected in that way; but that was the fashion in the early days of the Republic, before the evil days came upon us, and before the public service had become demoralized. The office used to seek the man, and not the man the office.

CONDITION OF PARTIES AT HIS ENTRANCE UPON PUBLIC LIFE.

CHARLES SUMNER was now forty years of age and in the first full strength of his intellectual manhood. He had appeared upon the national scene at an important conjuncture of public affairs. There were evidences on every hand of an approaching change in public sentiment and in the control of political parties. His own election had, indeed, been one of the most ominous portents of the coming revolution. The slavery question had entered the field of political action, and the old parties had already begun to be dashed to pieces upon that unyielding rock. The Whig party which had carried the country for Harrison in 1840, been defeated by its adversary in 1844, though led by Henry Clay, and again successful with Gen. Taylor in 1848, was the first to show signs of disintegration. The leaven of anti-slavery had largely entered this organization, especially in New England; but an attempt had been made in the party to suppress these anti-slavery tendencies, and this effort had the weight and sanction of the name and leadership of Daniel Webster, the great Whig orator and statesman.

The open rupture came in 1848, when the then immediate question of the prohibition of slavery in the new territories acquired in the Mexican war divided the party and led to the formation of what was called, with felicitous propriety, the "Free Soil party;" an organization composed of the seceding anti-slavery Whigs, of independent Democrats, and largely reinforced by the members of the "Liberty party," the pioneers of practical anti-slavery, an organization which had polled about seven thousand votes for Jas. G. Birney for President in 1840 and nearly seventy thousand for the same candidate in 1844. CHARLES SUMNER had, after vainly struggling to bring the Whig party of Massachusetts up to the anti-slavery standard, joined the new Free Soil party. It carried no State for Van Buren and Adams in 1848, but it polled more than a third of a million votes, and it was the forerunner of the great Republican party which was formed six years later, and which carried the country for Abraham Lincoln in 1860.

MR. SUMNER AN ANTI-SLAVERY MAN—HIS WATCHWORD.

CHARLES SUMNER had long been an anti-slavery man. With rare fidelity to conviction and to truth he had turned his back upon all apparent self-interest, upon all the professional and political prospects so inviting to a talented and ambitious young man, had at the same time resisted the still stronger blandishments and menaces of his aristocratic social surroundings, freely dedicating himself to the cause of the poor and oppressed, and braving the social and political ostracism of the rich and the powerful. But though an anti-slavery man, he believed in political action. Garrison, on the contrary, had taken the ground of disunion, and for his motto in the struggle, "*The Constitution is a league with death and a covenant with hell.*" CHARLES SUMNER took for his watchword, "FREE-

DOM NATIONAL—SLAVERY SECTIONAL," and kept that lofty political truth upon his banner until the battle was over. He believed and insisted that there was power enough under the Constitution to resist the spread of slavery and to bring back the Government to the anti-slavery ground held by the founders and early statesmen of the Republic.

A GLANCE AT MR. SUMNER'S CAREER IN THE SENATE—HIS ASSOCIATES AND LABORS.

Of MR. SUMNER'S career in the Senate I shall not speak in detail nor follow further his life in chronological order. His history since his entrance into public life has been a part of the history of the nation in its most important and tragic epoch; he has played his part in a high place and in the sight of all his countrymen, and if there were any need that the facts and incidents of his Senatorial career should be recounted, it has already been amply and sufficiently done in the thousand eulogies of press and tongue since his death. His early history was less familiar, and seemed a fitting and necessary introduction to a proper analysis of his public character.

Let me pass on, therefore, with only a glance at MR. SUMNER'S career in the Senate from that first day of December, 1851, when he took his seat in that historic chamber as the successor of Daniel Webster, the very day on which Henry Clay, the great Commoner of America, spoke his last word and left it forever, until the 10th day of March, 1874, when he, also, weary and worn with pain and disease, though not yet broken by age, his gray locks illustrious with service to his country and mankind, bade a pathetic though unconscious adieu to the great hall and went home to die. When he sat down in that Senate of 1851, with Cass, and Seward and Douglas for his associates, slavery and compromise ruled supreme. The senatorial seats were filled with haughty slave masters from the south and submissive politicians from the north, with two men only in the whole body who fully sympathized with him in his anti-slavery position and stood with him in that apparently forlorn hope of freedom,—the bold and ready John P. Hale, and Salmon P. Chase, afterwards the great Secretary and Chief Justice. Seward, it is true, was anti-slavery, but he was a Whig, and he had not yet broken with his party at the South.

In that body of slave-holders and slavery-supporters, SUMNER received no political or social recognition. He was assigned no place on the Committees, and when in the summer of 1852 he raised his voice for the first time in that splendid and memorable speech against the Fugitive Slave Law, he met the scornful and defiant glances of an enraged Senate. Other great speeches succeeded, arraigning Slavery at the bar of the public judgment and conscience. Then followed the murderous assault of Brooks, which planted physical, nervous torture in his frame and shortened his life. By-and-by came the war, and then, as the haughty representatives of slavery retired, SUMNER for the first time found himself with the majority and was entrusted with the practical direction of measures and policies. How he filled that important chairmanship which was then given him, until within recent years he was dismissed from it under circumstances of honor to him but of everlasting shame to those who did it. all the world knows. And all the while he was true to Freedom and the Union, never losing heart or hope. Finally, at the last, when the war had long been over and when the great work of reconstruction was finished, there came that separation from the administration of his party and from old political and personal friends, which tried anew his courage, and furnished the last severe test of his absolute obedience to his convictions of duty.

MR. SUMNER AS A STATESMAN—PECULIARITIES IN HIS CAREER.

In considering CHARLES SUMNER as a statesman, we are met at the outset by this striking peculiarity in his career: It was passed in the discharge of the duties of a single office, that of Senator from Massachusetts in the Congress of the United States. In this office, which has been filled by so many hundreds of undistinguished men since the foundation of the government, he performed his work and won his great fame. The man in our history who comes nearest to him in this respect is Thomas H. Benton, and he fails to furnish a parallel, for he had been a member of the other house of Congress. Most of our national statesmen of wide fame have filled different stations in the public service, and have had large opportunities and experiences. John Quincy Adams, whom SUMNER resembled in scholarship and integrity, filled almost the entire round of the chief offices under the government. Henry Clay, also, had a wide and diversified experience.

Still another peculiarity is found in the fact that SUMNER entered public life at the comparatively mature age of forty, and finished his career at sixty-three, an age which is not considered old among statesmen. Here, also, he differs from most eminent statesmen in this and other countries. William Pitt, the younger, entered Parliament at twenty-one; Gladstone at twenty-three; John Quincy Adams began his public career at twenty-seven; Henry Clay at twenty-nine; John C. Calhoun at twenty-eight, and Daniel Webster at thirty-two.

CHARLES SUMNER, therefore, was not fortunate in large opportunities, and his career, as we have seen, was not among the longest. Only was he felicitous in being privileged to act his part in our grand and stirring times. Here he had an opportunity worthy of his mature preparation and his commanding talents, and he improved it with sublime fidelity and courage. His is still another notable instance of that divine selection of men to serve and save great causes and interests at supreme moments and in national crises.

THE COLOSSAL POWER OF SLAVERY WHICH HE ATTACKED.

If we approach now to a view of the essential character of MR. SUMNER'S work as a statesman, we shall see that it was his mission to lead in the great effort for national regeneration; in lifting the nation up from slavery to freedom, and thus in serving it and saving it in the best and highest sense. We had this great evil of slavery in our political system, and from being at first an unfortunate exception it had come to be the rule in the administration of the government and in the general course of public opinion. It swayed and dominated alike over church and state, over pulpit and caucus. It laid its hand on the two great political parties of the country, and they made haste to do its bidding. Statesmen bowed their heads in the dust before it and trembled at its slightest frown. Its subtle and baleful influence permeated all public opinion and penetrated to every avenue and corner of society. All organizations of men, of whatever name or purpose, yielded unquestioning obedience to its lordly behests. Free speech was cowed into silence or pursued to martyrdom. The very springs and fountains of the popular thought and conscience were poisoned and corrupted. Nor did the sacred altars of religion escape the fearful contamination. Strange as it may seem now, even the churches of the land were made to uphold slavery, and the ghastly and blasphemous parodox was exhibited of defending "the sum of all villainies" in the name of the blessed gospel of peace, charity and liberty! The institution which was afterwards guilty of treason and rebellion against the government, thus began its work by insulting reason, stifling conscience and dethroning God in the souls of men.

I know it is difficult by any use of words, to make the generation which has come upon the stage since the war, realize the fearful sway and tyranny of the slave power in this country thirty years ago; and even the men who lived and acted then have almost forgotten in these days of liberty, when slavery has been in its grave ten years, the full strength and prevalence of that fearful moral, political and social influence which then ruled supreme. Some there are, the few survivors of that little band who composed the van-guard of the after swelling and triumphant hosts of freedom, who will perhaps remember the terrors of that collossal power against which they threw themselves with such uncalculating and heroic courage, in those dark days of the past. It was indeed, a time of moral and political paralysis. All true love of liberty, all genuine manhood, seemed expiring in the hearts of men. We know now that this was the thick, stifling atmosphere which presages the earthquake and the hurricane. Only the war with its flashing thunderbolts, was able to rend and lift those murky clouds, and let in once more the pure light and air of freedom.

It was against this dark institution of slavery, this gigantic public enemy, that MR. SUMNER waged unrelenting, unceasing war. Slavery had become the nation's master. Its firm grasp upon the nation's throat must be shaken off or the nation would die. SUMNER entered upon the stage in the days of expedients and compromises. The national capital was then, as it long had been before, the very fortress and citadel of oppression. The halls of Congress had long resounded to the apotheosis of slavery. Here his public career as a statesman commenced,—here in the very face of the enemy he began his work. He became the champion of imperiled freedom and the unrelenting foe of compromise. "FREEDOM NATIONAL—SLAVERY SECTIONAL"—"NO COMPROMISE WITH SLAVERY"—these were his watchwords.

THE CHAMPION OF AN IDEA IN STATESMANSHIP.

CHARLES SUMNER thus became the advocate and champion of an idea, a principle in statesmanship. It has often been said of him since, by way of criticism, that he was not a practical statesman; that he was not expert and crafty in the details of legislation. Let this be fully admitted and it falls far short of proving that MR. SUMNER was not a statesman of the best and highest type.

For certainly it must be the noblest business of a statesman to deal with principles and ideas, and he must be greatest in the service of the State who builds his superstructure upon these eternal foundations. I have no patience with that super-practical view of statesmanship which insists that he only is a statesman who shows aptitude and skill in the measures and policies of to-day. Undoubtedly, the affairs of to-day must be attended to, but they are not necessarily the most important. Statesmanship, like every other human interest, has its to-morrows; and these must be provided for. The rule here holds good in greater things as it does in lesser. The wise man builds his house upon a rock and makes careful provision for the future. So the wise statesman seeks to lay the beams of the national edifice on the solid and enduring foundations of eternal right and justice, and to provide wise rule for all after generations.

NOT A VISIONARY AND IMPRACTICABLE STATESMAN.

It is in this larger sense that I claim the highest meed of statesmanship for CHARLES SUMNER. He did great and far-reaching work. At the same time I confidently assert that he was a careful and sound legislator upon minor questions of state, evincing always an excellent judgment in what have been called practical, every-day affairs. I know the popular impression is the other way, but the popular impression has never been right upon this point. He was never wild or visionary. In the affair of the Trent he showed the highest prudence of diplomacy; he was sound always upon the finances. These instances are notable, but they are not the only ones that might be given to show that MR. SUMNER was not a rash or imprudent public man. But it was in the greater questions of State, where men did not see as far and as clearly as he, that he was called visionary and impracticable.

True, it was MR. SUMNER'S great work and distinction as a statesman to advocate an idea, a principle in government, rather than to manage a party or provide for the annual budget. But his idea was a grand one, his principle was an immortal one, and its effects on men and governments most powerful and practical. An idealist, men say. But what was his idea? Liberty, that great flame which has fired the hearts of men in all lands and ages; the quenchless inspiration of the heroes and martyrs of history; Liberty, the glory and felicity of nations which enjoy it, the undying aspiration of nations and peoples which seek after it. The best blood of the centuries has reddened field and scaffold for it; the most eloquent voices of the ages have pleaded in immortal words for this greatest boon of humanity. And is it not the best work of a statesman to seek to crystalize this beneficent principle into government, and to make it the sure possession of posterity?

THE CHARGE THAT HE WAS NOT A PRACTICAL STATESMAN DENIED—AN APPEAL TO THE RECORD.

The claim which I make here for MR. SUMNER'S statesmanship is justified by the great and beneficent results which have flowed from it. Not a practical statesman! Whose work has been more grandly practical than his? Look at it. Four millions of slaves emancipated and made freemen and citizens of the Republic. What could be more practical to them? The Republic itself at last rid of its greatest curse and most dangerous enemy; what could be more practical to it and to us? Liberty, Citizenship, Enfranchisement and Civil Rights; National Salvation and National Honor,—these are intensely practical things, and these are the objects which MR. SUMNER'S statesmanship compassed.

But it is said that he was impracticable. If by this it is meant that he was unmanageable by mere politicians and could not be induced to surrender principle for party, it is undoubtedly true. But if it be intended by this to say that as a statesman he proposed and advocated measures that could not be practically realized, or which were opposed to the true good of the country, then I confidently deny the charge and appeal to the facts to disprove it. What MR. SUMNER proposed and advocated in the Senate of the United States is well known to all the world. Let us look a monent at the record.

HIS STATESMANSHIP BEFORE THE WAR.

Take the questions which grew out of slavery and the war as the tests in this matter, for it was in these that he was said to be impracticable. His first speech in the Senate was in opposition to the fugitive slave law. He denounced it as unconstitutional, impolitic and inhuman. His vote was recorded against it. Was he not right in this? What man now would have the country go back and stand upon the fugitive slave law? Millard Fillmore signed that bill as President, and it was a millstone about his neck forever after. Which was right, the President or the Senator?

Then, MR. SUMNER opposed the repeal of the Missouri Compromise and the Nebraska bill, voting and protesting in some of his most powerful speeches against those ill-starred measures. Who questions now that it would have been better for the country and its peace to have left the landmark of freedom undisturbed? Stephen A. Douglass made here the mistake of his life; a mistake which cost him the presidency.

Next, MR. SUMNER voted and protested against the spread of slavery into the Territories, and lifted up his voice in one of his most memorable utterances in denunciation of the "Crime against Kansas,"—the daring attempt of slavery propagandists to plant slavery in that Territory by fraud and violence. Was he not right here? Let the memory of Franklin Pierce, whose administration was guilty of complicity in the crime, answer.

Then, in 1860, MR. SUMNER, gathering all his learning, ability and eloquence, from his high place in the Senate, arraigned the turbulent and threatening institution in that terrible indictment contained in his speech, entitled, "The Barbarism of Slavery." Here certainly he needs no vindication. All the world knows now that slavery was a relic of barbarism, and the very next year it added to its other crimes the greatest of all, and lighted the torch of civil war.

HIS RECORD DURING THE WAR.

When the war was impending, MR. SUMNER opposed the granting of the last concessions which slavery demanded of the North as the price of peace. He refused to compromise, and demanded that the government assert its just authority. Right again, clearly right. Concession would have been national humiliation, and peace thus purchased would have been national shame. Let the dishonored memory of James Buchanan, loaded down with the record of his criminal weakness, in a great crisis which demanded the will and courage of a man, testify to the clear, courageous and lofty statesmanship of CHARLES SUMNER, at this supreme moment of our history.

When the war came, MR. SUMNER was the first among our statesmen to urge the policy of emancipation. The policy was afterwards adopted, it is true, but not until hundreds of thousands of precious lives had been sacrificed, and hundreds of millions of treasure had been sunk. History, which has already vindicated the policy will, I think, write it down also, that MR. SUMNER was nearest right in point of time.

MR. SUMNER AND RECONSTRUCTION.

Then, after the war, followed the work of reconstruction. MR. SUMNER was again the first among all our statesmen to comprehend the full significance of the revolution which the war had effected and the great political changes which it had made necessary. He demanded and advocated for the emancipated millions, those measures which he denominated the "irreversible guarantees of freedom"—Citizenship, Enfranchisement, Civil Rights; these were the outlines of his policy.

I have not the time to go into the details here, as I would like; but the history is recent, and I simply call your attention to the fact that in every step of this policy of reconstruction and legislative dealing with the emancipated race, MR. SUMNER led the way, reluctantly followed, a year behind, by a Senate and Congress which continually denounced him as "impracticable." Year by year, the spectacle was presented of MR. SUMNER, at the opening of Congress, proposing measures which after being duly criticised and condemned as unreasonable and impracticable, were voted down by the majority only to be adopted at the next session or by the next Congress, when the wise and tireless champion had set his stakes still further ahead to be again denounced and again followed.

CRUEL DELAY OF HIS CIVIL RIGHTS BILL BY THE "PRACTICAL" STATESMEN.

It is a singular history and a sad commentary on what is called practical statesmanship. We spent ten years in this work of reconstruction and in adopting measures which MR. SUMNER proposed at the outset, and which are now clearly seen to have been necessary. Saddest of all, the jealousy and opposition of these laggards who are called "practical" statesmen finally cheated MR. SUMNER of what would have been the extreme felicity of his life. Even his great Civil Rights bill, the crowning measure of reconstruction and of his glorious career as a statesman, must be postponed by them until after his death. Oh, cruel delay! The death agony was made more intense by the thought, and this drew from the dying statesman that pathetic injunction to his friend, which so touched millions of hearts. How would that noble soul have thrilled with joy at the completion of the great work! The grand old warrior of Freedom could then have loosed his helmet, unbuckled his armor, and tasted the sweets of victory, on the field where he had fought so long.

What need that I should say more to prove that the charge, so often repeated, that MR. SUMNER was an impracticable and visionary statesman, is not founded in the truth of history. Happy would it have been for the government and the people if all our statesmen and public men had been as "practical" as he, and had followed his example and had recorded their votes and influence with him on these great questions to which I have referred. In every instance he is proved to have been right, and the practical statesmen to have been wrong. Thus time and history vindicate the truth and its champions. The "practical" statesmen are put to shame, their quibbling evasions and hollow compromises are exposed and overthrown, and the man who stood upon uncompromising truth is crowned with immortal honor, and again is vindicated in these greater things the old and homely maxim, "honesty is the best policy."

SAN DOMINGO AND THE BATTLE-FLAG RESOLUTIONS.

But I ought not to omit, in this connection, to speak of two important public questions where MR. SUMNER'S action subjected him, at the time, to wide-spread misapprehension and denunciation. I allude to the San Domingo annexation scheme and the battle-flag resolution.

His action on the first of these questions was taken in opposition to the administration of his own party, and subjected him to great personal annoyance and insult, finally leading to an open rupture with the President and a sundering of his party relations. Yet here he was clearly right, and his conduct in courageously opposing that ill-starred project was a signal service to his country, and worthy the highest admiration. For once he carried the country with him and defeated the measure. This certainly was "practical" statesmanship.

His battle-flag resolution was least understood of all his public acts, at the time, and subjected him to a perfect tempest of denunciation from the political friends of a life time. Even Massachusetts made haste to visit her public censure upon the head of her great, true son as he sat there in his darkened chamber at Washington, bowed with disease and suffering. It is the saddest story in MR. SUMNER'S life, and the blow was more cruel than that of Preston Brooks. The victim suffered in a silence that was heroic and grand. Thank God, the madness and misconception were only temporary. When reason returned, it was seen that the statesman was right and the people were wrong. Now, in all the land, the man could hardly be found to stand up and oppose the spirit and policy of MR. SUMNER'S resolution. Seldom is a vindication so speedy and overwhelming, and this is the last instance which I need to give of the practical wisdom of CHARLES SUMNER'S statesmanship.

"By their fruits ye shall know them" is a rule of the highest wisdom and authority, and as applicable to statesmen as to other men. Tried by this standard, MR. SUMNER is exalted among statesmen. A striking instance and contrast in our own history is in point.

SUMNER AND CALHOUN.

A year before CHARLES SUMNER'S election to the Senate, John C. Calhoun died at Washington, after a long and distinguished career in the councils of the nation. Like SUMNER he died a Senator and the greatest from his section. These two men will stand in our history as the fittest and ablest representatives of the North and the South, of Freedom and Slavery. They were both men of strong will, of unblemished private life and of commanding talents. As the sun of the great South Carolinian set, that of the Northern statesman arose. Massachusetts and South Carolina, the States that "shoulder to shoulder went through the revolution and felt the strong arm of Washington lean on them for support," furnished these two statesmen to the Union. As Slavery and the South found in Calhoun their ablest and most tireless senatorial advocate and statesman, so Freedom and the North at last had in SUMNER, in the same great arena, their most persistent and powerful champion. The one spent his life and his great talents defending human bondage and warring upon Freedom; the other as freely gave his great acquirements and noble faculties to the cause of freedom amd the slave.

Behold now how time and history have dealt with the two champions and the opposing systems which they defended. The doctrines of Calhoun ripened into secession and civil war to overthrow the government; those of SUMNER into emancipation, a restored Union and civil rights to all. The grim spirits of slavery and treason, of war and bloodshed, rise up at the name of Calhoun; upon the memory of SUMNER Freedom and white-winged Peace shed their sweetest benedictions, and millions of broken fetters are his trophies of victory.

MR. SUMNER AS AN ORATOR.

Plutarch, in comparing the two great orators of antiquity, says: "It is necessary, indeed, for a statesman to have the advantage of eloquence." This advantage MR. SUMNER possessed in a very eminent degree. He was indeed an orator of the classic type and of the most massive kind. Few, if any, modern parliamentary speakers have excelled him. Nature had done much for him in this respect. His personal presence was noble and commanding, and his voice, a deep and mellow bass, was sonorous and far-resounding. His temperament was not electrical, and hence he was never fiery or rapid in delivery, but spoke with judicial gravity with full articulation and with measured, impressive periods. He had the majesty and weight of manner which give such dignity to senatorial eloquence. It is a singular co-incidence that in these respects he more nearly resembled his great predecessor in the Senate, Daniel Webster, than any other modern orator.

His style partook of the qualities of his moral nature and of his personal presence. It was lofty in thought and purpose and stately in utterance. Not always flexible and never diffuse; sometimes, indeed, seeming stiff and lacking in euphony, it was always pitched upon a lofty key, and rose in volume and grandeur to the close. Here he most resembled Milton, to whom, indeed, there was still further resemblance in the grave and majestic expression of countenance, in vast and affluent scholarship, in lofty and severe integrity of life, and in unswerving devotion to the rights of man. It was a style admirably suited to the great themes of State which it became his mission to discuss. He was the advocate of Liberty, Humanity, Justice and Nationality, and he needed the highest dignity and power of speech to plead for these.

MR. SUMNER was not distinguished or dexterous in off-hand debate, but chose rather to advocate or oppose measures in full and well considered speeches. In this respect he was peculiar and, I think, unapproachable by any other statesman or orator we have ever had. His great speeches were so thoroughly prepared that they were exhaustive of the question and literally unanswerable. (History, literature, learning, logic and eloquence were gathered with a mighty sweep from far and near, and molded and welded in a great volume of argument, demonstration and persuasion which was absolutely overwhelming and irresistible.) No modern orator ever excelled him in this cumulative power. It is a singular fact that while his greatest senatorial efforts always provoked fierce opposition and called forth unmeasured personal denunciation, they were never answered. The orator was assailed with angry words, and even personal violence, but his speech was not replied to. And this was simply for the reason that it could not be replied to. An argument, founded on the truths of nature and history, with the adjuncts of all reason, learning and literature to support and fortify it, and fused and kindled by a sublime moral enthusiasm into a blaze of majestic eloquence, it was a power which could not be resisted in kind.

SUMNER AND EDMUND BURKE.

As a parliamentary orator, besides Webster, MR. SUMNER nearest resembled Edmund Burke. The men were not unlike in many respects, and the subjects upon which they spoke were not altogether dissimilar. Both had great resources of statesmanship, learning and eloquence; both spoke upon full preparation and exhaustively, and both denounced great public wrongs. SUMNER excelled Burke in delivery as much as he was excelled by the latter in style, which, for purity and richness of language, and imperial sweep of imagination, is still the study of rhetoricians and the model of statesmen. The speech of Burke in the British House of Lords, against the oppressor of India, and the speech of SUMNER in the American Senate, on the Barbarism of Slavery, are the two most remarkable and powerful philipics in the English language, and they will be read and ranked in times to come with their great originals, the orations of Cicero against Cataline and Verres, and of Demosthenes against Phillip. As Edmund Burke is the ornament and glory of English statesmanship and eloquence, so, I think, will CHARLES SUMNER hereafter be of American, for he had the high themes and the great purpose which will give his eloquence immortality.

MR. SUMNER NOT A POPULAR FAVORITE.

MR. SUMNER was never, in his life time, a popular public man. He had none of the arts of the demagogue, and his aims were always high above the multitude. It is one of the penalties of real greatness to be misunderstood and opposed. He was a statesman who followed the truth with a martyr's devotion, and he frequently received the martyr's reward. Men of lofty aims and uncompromising ways always make enemies. It will not answer to say that this is their fault. The multitude in all ages have stoned their prophets and crucified their benefactors. Even the noblest and greatest being that ever appeared in human form was surrounded at every step of his beneficent mission by enemies, who finally took his life. MR. SUMNER never asked favors of the people, and always opposed them when they were wrong. In this, of course, he was their truest friend, because he served their best interests. (For many years the purest and greatest of our statesmen, there was no time when his name could have commanded any considerable or formidable support for President, either in his party or before the people.) Not that the country did not need such men as he was for that office, but his great, pure life was a constant rebuke to the average smallness and meanness of politicians, and his courageous denunciation of popular wrongs had offended the easy-going complacency of the people. But happily, he never sought the Presidency, like so many of our public men, and he therefore suffered no disappointment.

I do not mean to say that a popular statesman or public man is always or necessarily unworthy. Notable instances in our own history would prove the contrary. A good man may represent or reflect the people in their best and highest moods and be popular with them, while at the same time he serves his country and secures an honorable name in history. In this way Lincoln was popular, because, a man of the people himself, he caught their inspiration and reflected their will at a great crisis, when they were at the white moral heat of revolution. But SUMNER led the way to national reform through popular opposition, prejudice and clamor, and spent his life in the advocacy of unpopular causes and ideas. Hence he could never be a favorite with the masses. Clay and Douglas were great party leaders and were idolized by their followers. They marshalled their forces like skillful generals and fought the battles of their day on the field of national politics. But they took the people as they found them, and left them little better. SUMNER, on the contrary, was not a politician or the leader of a party, but the bold proclaimer and champion of unpopular and unwelcome political truths, and he finally left the people, who reluctantly followed him, upon a higher plane of political knowledge, equality and liberty.

HIS ABILITIES OF THE FIRST ORDER.

The natural endowments of MR. SUMNER were large, and even in this respect, I think he was entitled to rank in the first order of statesmen. If he had not the vast brain and the intellectual affluence of Webster, he nevertheless was gifted by nature with a mind of uncommon strength, having the capacity for continued labor and acquisition and the blended moral and intellectual insight to direct it to great and noble achievement. In learning, whether useful or ornamental, in the knowledge of history and literature, so important to a statesman, he greatly excelled Webster, while in moral character and purpose he rose far above him. It is difficult to separate and lay apart the qualities of such a mind as MR. SUMNER'S, and to say how much was natural endowment and how much was acquired, for the very capacity to acquire and the moral inspiration to guide and direct the intellectual effort were equally the original gifts of nature. It is, therefore, useless to speculate in a matter of this kind. Enough that the full assemblage of of qualities and graces which made up the entire of MR. SUMNER'S moral and intellectual character were ample to entitle him to rank in the first order of publicists and statesmen. Washington, in spite of the celebrated aphorism of Henry Lee, has been excelled in war and peace alike, but never, perhaps, in the wonderful poise and balance of faculties which have made him one of the few romantic and legendary heroes of history.

Men of conspicuous lives, who play important parts upon the world's stage, whether warriors, rulers or statesmen, must be judged by what they do and what they are, and the measure of their greatness must be the impression which their work and influence makes upon their times, their nation and the world. Tried by this standard CHARLES SUMNER must be admitted into the immortal company of the world's great men. He was great as a scholar, orator and statesman, and exceptionally great in the moral qualities which he brought to statesmanship. History will be searched in vain to find another statesman who so steadily, unswervingly and consistently devoted his public life to truth, justice and freedom, and who sought with such zeal and courage to bring the Sermon on the Mount into the field of legislation and government. He was called "the Senator with a conscience," a term which truly described him while it indicated the contrast between him and so many other of our public men. Another title which in his last years, especially, he bore unquestioned, was that of "The Great Senator." How much that expresses, and how true it was! He towered intellectually above the dull commonplace of the Senate in these later, degenerate days, like the lofty peak of Teneriffe; or like Mont Blanc in the whiteness and majesty of his character.

HIS MORAL GREATNESS.

It is, indeed, in the moral greatness of his life that CHARLES SUMNER surpasses all our statesmen. This will constitute his chief distinction in history, for other statesmen have been learned, able and eloquent, but not one of all the great names our country can boast has so exalted statesmanship above the mere policies and expedients of to-day into the grand, clear region of eternal and immortal principles. Liberty and the equality of all men before the law—these were his guiding stars and the rule of his life.

HIS FIRMNESS AND CONSTANCY.

From these lofty purposes nothing could tempt him, nothing could swerve him. In the long anti-slavery struggle, his firmness and constancy never changed. What Martin Luther was at the Diet of Worms CHARLES SUMNER was, three hundred years later, in the American Congress. He stood as bravely and firmly for personal and political liberty as Luther did for liberty of conscience. Wendell Phillips once said that John Quincy Adams carried Plymouth Rock to Washington. This was even truer of SUMNER. A son of the Puritans himself, he stood for the truth as firm set and unshaken as Plymouth Rock, always and everywhere. When the hearts of other men grew faint in the long contest, when the clouds gathered and the heavens were dark above them and there was talk of compromise or surrender, the great leader never faltered or turned aside but kept straight on, his face to the foe, and his clarion voice ringing out words of lofty encouragement. He was indeed,

> "Constant as the Northern Star,
> Of whose true-fixed and resting quality
> There is no fellow in the firmament."

HIS INTEGRITY.

Need I speak of his integrity? In an age of venality in politics and of corruption among public men, he stood so conspicuously white in his character that no breath of suspicion, even, ever for a moment rested upon his name. What praise was that! All around him in these few, sad years which have gone, were the wrecks of character, his fellows in the public service broken, dishonored and disgraced, while he stood like a rock in the midst of the sea, giving his countrymen assurance still that all honor and integrity were not gone from the high places of the Republic. Alas, that he is now gone from the place where his example is so much needed!

HIS MORAL COURAGE.

And then, what lofty moral courage he had! Here he was sublime. We have seen that in his young manhood he put all the prospects of his life and of his ambition in peril for the cause of the slave. This was but the beginning, the dedication to a work which demanded of him ever after to face opposition, obloquy, slander, danger and death itself Oh! it has been easy in these recent years to be anti-slavery, to go with the majority, to swim with the tide, when the North has been all aroused, and when anti-slavery has been the passport to public office and public favor. But think what it was in the dark days when CHARLES SUMNER put on his armor and went forth like David against Goliath, to battle against the colossal power of Slavery.

Nor was it always or alone that he had enemies to face, as he did in the first half of his public life. In these later years he frequently had to brave the opposition and frowns of friends. To a lofty and sensitive soul this is the hardest of all. But even this could not daunt him. He met their cruel wrong and ingratitude as he had the rage of enemies.

I have no language to express my admiration for such courage as CHARLES SUMNER displayed throughout his entire public career. It was as rare as it was grand and heroic. It was the chivalry of statesmanship. The courage of war and the battle field pales before it. What is mere physical bravery in comparison! To charge on serried lines or flaming batteries, in the shock and fury of battle, when the blood is mounting and hot with the fiery contagion of thousands all around, and the splendid intoxication of war drowns all thought of danger—this is the physical courage of the soldier, which the world in all ages has admired and applauded. But to stand alone, if need be, against the world, for a cause or an idea, to endure the sneers, the scorn and the scoffs of men;

to put reputation, character, prospects all at hazard for a principle —this is moral courage, this is courage which is Godlike and sublime!

HIS DEATH—THE UNIVERSAL TRIBUTE—WHO SHALL TAKE HIS PLACE?

The grand old patriot and statesman is at rest now. No more strife and opposition, no more weariness and pain, no more cruel wrong and ingratitude. He died as he had lived. There was no weakness, no obscuration of intellect, no unmanly fear of death. His sun went down like the full orb of day, with no clouds about its setting. How fitting here the noble passage from Milton:

> "Nothing is here for tears, nothing to wail
> Or knock the breast, no weakness, no contempt,
> Dispraise or blame, nothing but well and fair
> And what may quiet us in a death so noble."

All men honor his memory. The same fickle and ungrateful people who kill their prophets, build sepulchres and monuments to them after they are dead. And so in all the land, as in the whole wide circuit of civilization, nothing but good is said of the great Senator. All races and sections speak with the same voice. Next to the noble tribute of that brilliant Senator who was the great man's friend and associate, and who, though of foreign birth, speaks our language with such marvelous fluency and grace, there have been laid upon the statesman's bier no finer offerings than from those two men of the South, one the representative of the emancipated slave, the other of the once lordly slave master. Happy coincidence! Auspicious omen! Thus the wide gap closes between master and slave, between North and South; thus is the problem of statesmanship solved, and thus does a great life-work for common country and common humanity meet with its sure and glorious reward.

Thank God, there is appreciation and honor yet in America for a great, true man. As truly now can it be said as when Daniel Webster said it of Adams and Jefferson, that "The tears which are shed and the honors which are paid when the defenders of the Republic die, give hope that the Republic itself may be immortal." Well may the people mourn. Just as we are approaching our hun-

dreth national anniversary, our greatest and noblest statesman, the most august and commanding presence in our national councils is removed. Where shall we look for his like? The strong tower is, indeed, fallen. As our eyes sweep enquiringly around the political horizon, we see no one to take his place. And well may Massachusetts, once the proud mother of so many statesmen, weep for her buried greatness. Her long and illustrious line in the national Senate ends with him, her purest and her greatest, the light and glory of whose splendid name and services only make more palpable and dark the void which is left.

HIS PLACE IN HISTORY.

CHARLES SUMNER'S place in history is secure. Allied to immortal principles, to conscience and to God, his fame will live as long as the records of civilization shall endure. Liberty will enroll him with her immortal advocates and defenders; Eloquence will point to him as one of her noblest orators, and Humanity will enshrine him with her great benefactors. He will be the hero statesman; and as the noble knight of Liberty he will ride down the centuries. For he went forth with more than knightly courage, not to rescue from heathen profanation the earthly sepulchre where the Lord's body lay, but to save from the profaner hands of tyrannyand oppression millions of human souls in which the Lord's spirit now dwells.

As the statesman who led in the great effort which finally rid the Republic of the New World from the curse of African slavery he will keep company in history with Washington the founder and Lincoln the liberator; and in after ages when accurate historical narrative begins to blend with legend and tradition, a halo will surround his name like that which glorifies the names of Sidney and Hampden, of Bayard and Bozzaris and other illustrious defenders and martyrs of country and liberty. Thus do such lofty souls become the guardian angels of their country as the traditionary fame of William Tell hovers like a protecting aegis above the mountains of Switzerland. And such is the transfiguration which God vouchsafes to his great ones who help to lift humanity up to knowledge, to liberty and to Him.

www.ingramcontent.com/pod-product-compliance
Lightning Source LLC
LaVergne TN
LVHW011138110826
845150LV00008B/2390
* 9 7 8 1 4 1 8 1 9 3 1 1 9 *